Merma
Twisted Fates

Louise Cox

/ BookLeaf
Publishing

Presentation by *BookLeaf Publishing*

Web: www.bookleafpub.com

E-mail: info@bookleafpub.com

ISBN: 9789357691000

First edition 2022

ACKNOWLEDGEMENT

Thank you to those who help me remember the things forgotten.
Jaclyn Cherie you are an inspiration and Ian Cox for his patience with my fractured soul.

PREFACE

In search of meaning to stitch back together the fabric of a moth eaten tapestry of memories.

Don't

Don't daydream,
don't dance,
don't talk to the birds.
Whisper to trees
or converse with worms.
Don't pick up that stone
or shell or feather.
Dance in the rain, barefoot,
laughing with the weather.
Don't sing to the sun
or stay up sharing secrets with the moon.
Don't do any of these things
and soon.
The freedom and magic of childhood is lost.

Forgotten

Hidden in the thicket of my soul,
nesting in the moss.
All things forgotten
but never to be lost

Mermaid

Prussian blue, deep velvet night,
diamond studded stars shine bright.
The pregnant moon hangs low,
reflected on the sea,
waves caress the shore
with their haunting melody.
In the distance the Mermaids wait
anticipating the nights Fate.
Longing burns within their souls,
to drink the magic that a man holds
and when the moon is positioned just right.
They shed their tails
and walk onto the land for one night.
To seek a man pure of heart
who's love can carry them through the dark.
Emotions surging in their veins,
eyes wide and tempting,
set a blaze.
They wander down into town,
to see if there are any lost souls to be found.
On slender limbs not used to land,
seaweed gowns cling to
luminous forms.
Exquisite beauty
hair flowing down to her waist,

she spies a man
and smells the air to taste
if he might,
be her lover for one night.
Eyes glow with pure delight,
tasting the divine soul
she has in her sight.
Striding over to where he stands,
she moves in closer and takes his hand,
pressing it against her cheek.
They lock eyes and her soul is complete.
For in his eyes of blue,
she sees the source of all the seas converging.
A thousand years and more she's yearned,
for the moonlight to be right
to steal a kiss upon this night.
As her lips are pressed to his
she dives into his soul
and swims deep into his bliss.
For if a Mermaid is to exist
she needs to devour the magic
that emanates from a perfect kiss.

Capricious Stars

A glimmering star of hope,
a pin prick of light
in the vast blackness of despair
but stars are capricious things,
you can't always see.
You want to believe in wishes and dreams
but they vanish all too quickly,
after burning a hole in your soul
that the blackness rushes in to fill.

Past Path

When chaos rules a haunted moon,
fate deals a loaded hand.
Fragments of memories lost,
splintered lives a thousand years past,
intrude and intersect
upon the present path.

Thwarted by Fate

Can Fate be twisted to take another path.
Change destiny, alter my stars.
Try as I might,
Fate twists back and blocks my path.
I've tried diversion, denial, indifference.
Defiant I stand and declare my intention.
The Devil laughs.
As I try to dodge,
Fate twists back and blocks my path.
There must be a solution,
missing piece of the puzzle.
To break the unbreakable bond of Fate.
I pray to the Gods to give me a clue,
from past or future to interpret the present.
The Devil laughs.
As once again,
Fate blocks my path.

Aftermath

The aftermath of fear and anxiety saturates my cells.
Dark heavy pools refuse to drain away.
When you cannot run but have to stay.

Loss

Sadness engulfed me
and dragged me down
to the depths of my soul.
Grief, betrayal and salty tears
stain my cheeks
and mark my bones
with indelible loss.

I waited for the rain

I waited for the rain,
to cry with me.
Storms to blow my worries
out to sea.
I waited for the rain
to wash away the fear.
Winds to blow hurt
through branches taken with the leaves.
I waited for the storm to end
while the rain cried with me.

At the Cliffs edge

Standing at the edge of the cliff,
looking out to sea.
Let the wind pass through my thoughts
carrying them with the clouds.
Disperse them with the rain
to be filtered through the ground.

Battle torn

Battle torn her wounded soul,
lay forlorn at the edge of time.
Eons past her by
Spangled starlight kissed her skin
Luminous moon as if lit from within
Firefly dances across the sky
Eons past her by

Raven

A Raven dancing in the wind,
playing with the freedom
beneath her wings.

Freedom Breathes

Into the twilight
under the moon.
Twisted Fates bind my soul.
Tear out my heart,
untether my soul.
Bury them deep
in the sweet smelling moss.

Let my soul sleep.

Earth heal my spirit
and relight my soul
Stitch back my heart
to make me again whole.

As the sun rises and breaks into dawn,
the first shafts of light warm the soil
New blooms emerge
and push through the ground

Leaving the hurt and betrayal and loss
tangled up to sleep in the moss.
I raise my face to the light of the sun
Kiss Fate on the cheek
and tell him it's done.

As the sun rises higher
a new day begins
Song of the Blackbird
floats in the wind.
Out in the sunshine
to dance on a breeze,
lightest of feather
freedom breathes.

She dares to love

Although shards of betrayal penetrate her heart
Still
She dares to love.

Moonlit clouds

Moonlit clouds
sail past my window,
beckoning dreams
of dark pastel blue.

Shapeshifter

Shapeshifter, shadowself
I call on you tonight.
Raven winged, dragon clawed
eyes embers of ice.
Darkest protectoress
ready to take flight.
Chase away the demons,
hunt down our foes.
Terrifying, battlecry
penetrate their souls.
Return to me in morning light,
when all is done.
Let them heed this warning
Stay away, leave well alone
Or else this dreamwalker might
Send a fearsome dragon
to devour you in the night.

Shadows

Staring into the gaps in-between
we find the things which cannot be seen.
Dwelling in the bushes in the garden
and the hedgerows in the fields.
The Shadows
Am I watching them
or are they watching me.
Darker than the blackest night,
with sparkling eyes that twinkle
with the light of stars
burning bright.

Seaweed Sorceress

Seaweed tangled in her hair
mesmerising haunting stare.
The Seaweed Sorceress
weaves her spell.
Manipulate her twisted Fate,
break the bonds
that bind her
at the gate
of space and time.
Gambling against the Gods,
she'll turn her Fate
against all odds.

Ancestors

I woke up one night and in the pitch black,
the room was full of my ancestors
having a chat.
"What are you doing here,
please let me get through?"
As I pushed myself past them to get to the loo.
When I came back they were all still there.
"Really" I said
"your having a party here!"
"I'm going back to bed I need to sleep,
please let yourselves out when your ready to
leave".